Paolo Ruffilli

LIKE IT OR NOT

translated by

Ruth Feldmann & James Laughlin

Bordighera Press

Library of Congress Cataloging-in-Publication Data

Ruffilli, Paolo, 1949–
   (Piccola colazione. English & Italian)
   Like it or not / Paolo Ruffilli ; translated by Ruth Feldmann & James Laughlin.
      p. cm. -- (Crossings   ; v. 15)
   English and Italian
   ISBN 1–884419–75–5
   I. Feldmann, Ruth. II. Laughline, James, 1914– III. Title. IV. Series; Crossings (West Lafayette, Ind.)   ; v. 15.

PQ4878.U26P5313 2005
851'.914--dc22

2005055319

© 2005 by Paolo Ruffili, Ruth Feldman, and James Laughlin.
First published: June 2007

All rights reserved. Parts of this book may be reprinted only by written permission from the author and translators, and may not be reproduced for publication in book, magazine, or electronic media of any kind, or produced on stage, except in quotations for purposes of literary reviews by critics.

Printed in the United States.

Published by
BORDIGHERA PRESS
John D. Calandra Italian American Institute
25 W. 43rd Street, 17th Floor
New York, NY 10036

CROSSINGS 15
ISBN 1-884419-75-5

Contents

Piccola Colazione (1974—1986)	6
Malaria	8
Was It True Glory?	28
Like It or Not	48
The Siege of Constantinople	68
Notable Results	88
Outside the Body	118
About the Author and Translators	145

Indice

Piccola colazione (1974—1986)   7

Malaria   9

Fu vera gloria? 29

Per amore o per forza 49

L'assedio di Costantinopoli 69

Prodotti notevoli 89

All'infuori del corpo 119

Piccola colazione (1974–1986)

per Laura e Giulia

The void is a fabric painted with words. The words dye the void and, as on silk, they imprint colors and elegant shapes and, covering it again in this way, they become fixed little by little, until they remain, they alone, indelible.
— *Yukio Mishima*

Through the very fact that we speak, each thing is not what it is. The symbol is the murderer of the thing.
—*Jacques Lacan*

The word, for me,
came from far away .
I felt it to be almost
an *a priori*. A stimulant .
By a process in
some way inverse.
In giving it by comparison
a reality that, instead,
the more it was touched and grasped,
the more it fled
insubstantial
from the five senses.
With the effect of being
hurled against a body,
pronounced, and then,
in the pronouncing, suddenly
grasped again.

Piccola colazione (1974–1986)

per Laura e Giulia

Il vuoto è una stoffa dipinta di parole. Le parole tingono il vuoto e, come una seta, imprimono colori e figure eleganti e, così ricoprendolo, si fissano poco alla volta, fino a quando rimangono, ormai esse sole, indelebili.
— *Yukio Mishima*

Per il fatto stesso che si parla, ciascuna cosa non è quella che è. Il simbolo è l'assassino della cosa.
— *Jacques Lacan*

La parola, per me,
veniva da distante.
Un a priori, quasi,
l'avvertivo. Un eccitante.
In un processo in
qualche modo inverso.
Nel darle per riscontro
una realtà che invece,
più toccata e presa, più
sfuggiva inconsistente
ai cinque sensi.
Con l'effetto di essere
lanciata contro un corpo
pronunciato e, nel
suo dirlo, di colpo
riafferrato.

MALARIA

"Which is dearer, the name or the body?"
 — Lao-Tzu

"The highest degree of presence is absence."
 —Walter Benjamin

"It's too easy
to do what pleases
and what we want."

The small tin box
is round , and rolls
on side against the other.
You can smell it,
if empty, and lick the shell
when the licorice is gone.

Apple orange plum
Apple orange plum

...where do dreams spring from
clothes and profiles
to monster, to madness :
milkshakes and puzzles
whose pieces don't fit right,
like birds, their colors bright,
or huddledbats
that suddenly break off
the ink-blue tree.

Malaria

«Qual è più caro, il nome o il corpo?»
— *Lao-tzû*

«Il più alto grado di presenza è l'assenza».
— *Walter Benjamin*

«Troppo comodo
fare quello che piace
e che si vuole».

La scatola di latta
è tonda e ruota,
una parte sull'altra.
Si può odorarla, vuota,
e leccarla, quando
la liquerizia è terminata.

mela arancia susina
mela arancia susina

… da dove saltano
fuori, i sogni,
vesti e contorni
al mostro, alla pazzia:
frullati, puzzle con
i tasselli fuori posto,
come uccelli colorati
o pipistrelli
staccatisi di colpo
dall'albero blu inchiostro.

"It has to be a plot
grownups dream up
out of jealousy or spite."

From the impregnable tower
of one's own castle
from which everything else is kept
under strict control .
A kingdom that small
but safe and quite secure,
at least as long as we make sure,
the door is locked.

(Balancing undressed
on the bathtub edge,
he stares and seeks
the form, into the mirror,
or only a reason
for the fire
of so much desire.)

judge your stride and easy stand
throw the stone with steady hand
stop now or go to a far-off land

"My mother says I can
take off the clothes."
"Mine says not more than
my pants and undershirt."

(To see oneself and to be seen.
To lay it bare.
To hold it up, if it needs to be held.
But he believes inside himself

«Dev'essere un accordo
dei grandi,
per dispetto o gelosia».

Sulla torre del castello
inespugnabile, sicura
da cui si tiene il resto
sotto mira. Un regno
piccolo ma certo, per
il tempo almeno in cui
la porta è chiusa a chiave.

(Scruta, salito
sul bordo della vasca
in bilico, svestito,
indaga sullo specchio
la forma o una ragione
di tanto desiderio.)

pesa il passo e posa piano
lancia il sasso con la mano
ferma adesso o vai lontano

«Mia madre dice che
posso togliermi tutto».
«La mia, non più dei
pantaloni e della maglia».

(Vedersi, essere
visto. Metterlo a nudo.
Tenerlo, se deve essere
tenuto. Ma gli pare

there must be
something else.)

Red. The red of fever,
of blood. Into the fire.
Of nails and lips.
Of godless people.
Of capes and flags.

Aboard the submarine, "Me",
course set for the sea.
"Clear the deck,
secure the hatch.
Dive, dive fast."
The limited space
sackful of smells
shadow of the bed.

"...nest, table, heart
roof, soma, dwarf."

Again. Precise the dry old
rigmarole, word by word
in all its whole. Mirror
portrait, analogy and proof
that the thing is there :
it always will be,
always has been,
not everywhere
and as may be. Dictation.

che debba esserci
qualche altra cosa…)

Rosso. Di febbre, di
sangue. Dentro al fuoco.
Di unghie e labbra.
Di gente senzadio.
Di cappe, di bandiere.

Nel sommergibile, «Io»,
in rotta per i mari.
«Tutti sottocoperta,
chiudere i boccaporti.
Immersione rapida».
Lo spazio circoscritto
la sacca degli odori
l'ombra del letto.

«… cuore, desco, nido
gnomo, soma, tetto».

Ancora. Esatta
la secca tiritera
parola per parola.
Specchio, ritratto
analogia, prova
che c'è, sotto, la cosa:
quel che sempre sarà
e sempre è stato,
non dovunque e
come sia. Dettato.

... in the *Book of
Famous Books*,
in the encyclopedia.

"It has the colors
of fire, of snow
and grass."

"Come on, the game of forfeit is this :
to say, to do, or maybe kiss."

(Doing it again he seems
to like it more than before.
But he has the feeling that
if he stays so thin as a pin
it night be for this sin.)

"You'll see :
the faster you go,
the better it will be."

...that a word
has sex and person (male
if it ends with *a*!). But
harder to conceive
the state of want,
of absence, in short
the denied presence
in a concept not even
rejected, inconceivable,
of *nothingness*, and the wonder
to pronounce it.

... sul *Libro dei
Libri Famosi,*
nell'enciclopedia.

«... ha i colori
del fuoco, della neve
e del prato».

«Dai, paga il pegno.
Dire, fare, baciare,
lettera o testamento?».

(Non è che smetta
anzi, a rifarlo, gli
sembra anche più bello.
Però, ha il dubbio
che se resta magro
è proprio per quello.)

«Più vai veloce e
più, vedrai, ti piace».

 che una parola
abbia un sesso e una
persona (maschile se
finisce in *a*!). Ma
incomprensibile di più
lo stato di mancanza
di assenza, insomma
la parvenza negata
in un concetto neppure
rifiutato, inconcepibile,
del *niente* e lo stupore
a pronunciarlo.

"Where is it hers?
What is it made of ?"

(For him, only the joy
of being held. And
then the thought
that it's not fair
and not so much for her
after all, if she
doesn't have a thing.)

"You'll find it out
when you grow up."

Glimpsed in secret and said
in private, whispers
in the dark, indefinite
shapes and never clear,
clues to signals seized
in haste and fury
spelled, in fear
of getting found out
before laying bare
square inches
of crevices and down.

*Peter Piper picked a peck
Of pickled pepper...*

Fear that a glass may shatter,
salt scatter,
boiling water overflow
a gypsy enter home

«La sua, dov'è?
Da cosa è fatta?».

(A lui il gusto, solo,
di essere preso. E
il pensiero che è
ingiusto e svantaggioso,
e non tanto per lei
in fondo, se non ce l'ha.)

«Lo imparerai, quando
sarai più grande».

Visto in segreto e detto
al chiuso, in ombra
bisbigli, incerti
i margini, mai esatti
indizi di segnali
colti, strappati
in fretta e furia
a sillabe, per paura
di essere scoperti
prima di scoprire
centimetri quadrati
di anfratti, di peluria.

una rana nera e rara
sulla rena errò una sera

Paura che un vetro venga rotto
che il sale vada sparso
che si rovesci l'acqua mentre bolle
che una zingara entri in casa

the bottle of oil fall,
his health fail.
Fear of staying in the dark,
finding a murdered in his home,
losing an eye on a sharp spike,
not passing the exam as he'd like,
falling into a ravine,
ending by drowning in a lake,
being crushed to a mush.

"...you said it.
Already if you thought it
in little amount,
that it hasn't been
doesn't count."

"Will you join us, then?
Come on, let's talk dirty."
"We have to say
all nasty words."

Said and looked up
in the dictionary.
Accepted, therefore, shown
not totally unknown.
And the others, synonyms, more gray
with no features of their own
at least set down.

"This is the way they lie
on top, one of the other."

(Sprawled on the bed,
rehearsing the part with the pillow.

che cada il fiasco d'olio
che si rovini la salute.
Paura di restare al buio
di trovare in casa un assassino
di cavarsi un occhio su una punta
di non essere promosso
di cadere in un burrone
di finire dentro a un lago
di annegare, di essere schiacciato.

«... l'hai detto.
Già se l'hai pensato,
che non sia stato,
non conta più».

«Ci stai allora?
Dai, parliamo male».
«Dobbiamo dire
tutte parolacce».

Detti e guardati
sopra il dizionario.
Ammessi, dunque, o
non del tutto ignorati.
E gli altri, sinonimi
più amorfi e grigi,
almeno registrati.

«Si mettono così,
l'uno sull'altra».

(Sdraiato, a letto,
per l'ennesima prova
generale col cuscino.

Feverish, panting to do it right,
kissing and clutching it tight.)

One looking-glass
In front of another small,
moving it up and down
to check, back and fro
which is the new effect
of a different view.

"You shouldn't run around
with those good-for-nothings."

It may be true:
a trap for you
to tempt into sin
and make you fall in,
then caught in the snare,
doomed forever
among shrieks and cries
down in a lake, a ditch,
deep in a fire of pitch.

"What is confessed is taken away,
resolved. You're free
once you're absolved."

(Suddenly on a whim,
the idea torments him
that he doesn't , for sure,
match the idea of purity
that he was raised with.)

Febbrile e ansante
baciandolo, abbracciato.)

Contro lo specchio
rispetto a un altro,
piccolo, che scende e
sale, a controllare
qual è l'effetto
di una diversa visuale.

«Non devi stare
con certi mascalzoni».

Che sia davvero
proprio il tranello,
quello per tentarti
per farti cadere
e, preso nella rete,
condannato in eterno

tra urli e grida
nel lago, nella fossa
in mezzo al fuoco.

«Ciò che è confessato
è tolto. E resti libero
una volta assolto».

(Lo tormenta, a un
tratto, l'idea sgomenta
di non rispondere affatto
al modello di purezza
cui l'hanno abituato.)

...that he'll blurt out
a blasphemy without
meaning to, that
it might be forming in his mind
like a bomb primed
to go off any time.

Sure, whoever has gone
to seven first-Fridays of the month
though living not right,
prayers and litanies every night,
he will be saved
no matter what he has done
or keeps doing still.

"Meanwhile, God sees you,
of course, everywhere."

(He points there
before he is aware
by instinct is drawn
and sucked, meanwhile, his hand
to her convexity
without grip.)

"I'm going to tell your mother
you keep felling me up."

...let it happen then
and doesn't matter how,
let all restraint
be lifted, yes, at last
and, whatever the cost,
let what will be, be.

… che esca fuori
una bestemmia
senza volerlo, che
si formi in testa
per un innesco
incontrollato.

Ma, sì, chi è stato
ai sette primi venerdì
del mese, preghiere
e litanie per ogni sera,
qualunque cosa ha fatto
e che continua a fare
sicuramente è salvo.

«Intanto, dappertutto
Dio ti vede».

(Punta là, senza
saperlo. È attratto
per istinto, risucchiata
la sua mano, intanto,
a quel convesso
senza appiglio.)

«Lo dico a tua madre
che mi tocchi».

… che accada e
non importa come,
che finalmente
sia tolta ogni riserva
e, costi quel che costi,
si abbia il seguito.

In spite of the thought
of disgust, even in the stink,
in the seat, in the blood.

"Don't worry,
she likes it too."

To be done quickly
in the dark, behind
the room's closed doors,
so no one can know or see,
in secret, stealthily,
to someone's detriment
a risk, a offense
what's more a shame,
profaning as you must
the trust.

…it is, it proves to be
inconsistent,
the more it's claimed,
ordered, required,
against the standing
firm and deaf, the same
imperious and urgent
of its name.

Once more repeated
out loud or in his mind
putting it down again
long lines in notebooks,
in large or small letters
cursive or block capitals,

Nonostante l'idea
magari di disgusto,
anche nel sangue
nel puzzo e nel sudore.

«Piace anche a lei,
non credere».

Da consumarsi in fretta
al buio, al chiuso
della stanza,
senza che si veda o
che si senta, di nascosto
di straforo, a danno
di qualcuno, come offesa
rischio e, più, vergogna
violando, meglio che
si possa, la consegna.

… ed è, risulta
inconsistente,
quanto più detto
ordinato e richiesto,
contro lo stare
fermo e sordo, questo
sì imperioso e urgente,
del suo nome.

Di nuovo ripetuto
tra sé o a voce alta
riscritto in lunghe
file sui quaderni,
in grande e in piccolo
corsivo o stampatello

in the Greek alphabet
in the oldest style
drawn, even chiselled:
the same name.

"You don't do that
to a girl you like."

That she is damned,
impure and dirty
and lost...still meant
to be a lure
to quench a tempting thirst,
for just this thing
so painfully desired.

(He dreams to lose himself,
to fall into the arms
of a woman who's
utterly without scruples.)

"They let you do
whatever appeals to you."

To spell it out, clasped
to another, straining
on the borders, voice almost
pitted, clipped speech
between the teeth
like under a sheath
in a desperate puff of breath:
nothing more, just...*whore.*

in alfabeto greco
con la grafia più antica
disegnato, perfino
cesellato. Sempre quello.

«A una cui vuoi bene
non lo fai».

Che sia dannata, sì,
e impura e lurida
perduta… ma destinata
a spegnere una sete
appetitosa, proprio
per questa cosa,
dolorosamente desiderata.

(Il sogno suo è di
perdersi, di cadere tra
le mani di una donna
senza scrupoli.)

«Si fanno fare
quello che ti pare».

Da compitare, legato
a un altro, spingendo
sui contorni, a voce quasi
spenta, smozzicata
sotto ai denti come
sotto la sottana,
il soffio disperato
di… *puttana*.

Was It True Glory?

"The shape of the house is the course of a destiny.
Bunker, fort, decorous make : the typologies,
together, of a war and of the court. Prisoners and
jailers spy on the world from loopholes, and they
picture it to themselves in dreams."
— *Anonymous*

"The only truth that people accept is one
presented already digested and manipulated,
shrunken and adorned."
— *Herman Hesse*

"Come on ...
there's nothing on."

"...that's all for today.
We wish you goodnight."

Yes, the wonderful colors
of video,
the pleasant random choosing,
sipping, savoring
the flavor of soft dessert.
Grasping life
                      seasoned before,
pre-chewed and digested like this.
Surrendering to the game
of statues, to the neutral glossy
motion

Fu vera gloria?

«La forma della casa è il percorso di un destino. Bunker, fortilizio, labirinto decoroso: le tipologie, insieme, della guerra e della corte. Carcerati e carcerieri spiano il mondo dalle feritoie, e se lo rappresentano nel sogno».
— *Anonimo*

«L'unica verità che la gente accetti è quella presentata già come digerita e manipolata, rimpicciolita e decorata».
— *Hermann Hesse*

«Ma come, via... Non
danno proprio niente».

«... anche per oggi
abbiamo terminato.
Buone notte».

Sì, la splendida cromia
                           del video,
il dolce stare alla ventura
a prendere, sorbire, a degustare
i morbidi dessert.
A cogliersi la vita
                     già condita,
così, premasticata e digerita.
Per consegnarsi al gioco
delle pose, al neutro moto
patinato

                              in which
nothing really exists any more,
at a distance
                    that entertains
only for that little bit
that one is touched by it.
The same prearranged fantasy,
outside itself, hatched,
hypnotized, melted down.
The water
                    is held back no longer
it's a surge that floods, drowns,
swallows you down.

"When I was your age
I didn't have the time
to get bored."

The living room
is English style.
Fringes and tassels
everywhere. Knick-knacks
on every surface, prints
of flowers and castles.

(When it comes to himself,
he likes his hands the best,
enjoys looking at them more than the rest,
pretending to be in front.
Languid and slim,
they look almost feminine to him.)

"You and all your crazy plans...
Get your act together,

    in cui
più niente esiste veramente,
in una lontananza
       che intrattiene
ma per quel tanto solo
che uno sia sfiorato.
La stessa predisposta fantasia,
fuori di sé, covata
si ipnotizza, si dissolve.
Più non trattiene
       l'acqua
è un fiotto che dilaga
che affoga, che si ingoia.

«Alla tua età, io non
l'avevo, il tempo
per la noia».

Il salotto
è stile inglese.
Frange e fiocchi
dappertutto. Cocci
sui piani, stampe
di fiori e di castelli.

(Di sé, predilige
le mani.
Gli piace guardarle,
fingendosi di fronte.
Abbandonate e esili
quasi femminili.)

«Con tutti i tuoi progetti strani…
Ma tirali, i fili,

decide what you
would like to do."

Just beyond the shore
close to the surface
something comes in and out,
appears and disappears.
Leaving us in doubt
whether it exists for real
or is a trick,
an alibi, an excuse
the rest of a story
never set in motion
the rotten core
of an abortion.

"No matter what I say
I'm always wrong..."

(It may be because of his
skeptical and intolerant nature,
his laziness and levity
his narrow smartness,
maybe out of whim,
although fine qualities in him,
signs of thoughtful openness,
but he avoids talking if he can
on the edge of thoughts
behind the glow and smoke
that they evoke.)

"...he was killed
on the street, in front
of his house, by two boys
who rode off on a bike."

di quello che vuoi fare».

Appena oltre la riva
a pelo d'acqua
emerge e non emerge
pare e non pare.
Lasciandoci nel dubbio
se esista per davvero
o sia un inganno
un alibi, un pretesto
il resto di una
storia mai avviata
la noce putrefatta
di un aborto.

«Qualunque cosa dica,
ho sempre torto...».

(Sarà per l'indole
scettica e insofferente,
per la pigrizia e per la levità
per un'astuzia riduttiva
magari per capriccio,
del resto aspetti nobili, segni
d'apertura contemplativa,
ma si sottrae se può
all'uso di parole,
sul filo dei pensieri
dietro l'alone e il fumo
che essi lasciano.)

«... è stato ucciso
in strada, sotto casa,
da due giovani
scappati su un motore».

"Would you believe it? How
awful! The cowards!"

"Everyday is like this.
Give me the dishes."

"Hello. Who speaking ?
He's not here. He isn't back yet."

(Strange...
but when he sits down to eat
if there have been no deaths,
catastrophes or disasters,
well, he must admit
he feels let down a bit.)

"What about that money ?
Did you ask for it ? Are they going
to give it to you ?"

The table occupies
the whole dinette:
there's barely space
for the chairs.
And close at hand
there's a TV stand.

"See, if you get mad
it's only your fault."

(He realizes with pleasure
that he's still and always will be
what he once was,
always the same : a child

Like It or Not • 34

«Ma guarda lì, che
roba. Che vigliacchi».
«Ogni giorno così.
Passami i piatti».

«Pronto. Chi è?
Non c'è. Non è tornato».

(Fa un certo che...
ma quando sta mangiando,
se non ci sono morti
catastrofi e disastri,
ebbene sì lo ammette
a lui dispiace.)

«Quei soldi, allora
hai chiesto? Te li danno».

Il tavolo occupa
il tinello:
c'è posto appena
per le sedie.
E c'è un carrello
con il televisore.

«Se te la prendi, vedi
la colpa è solo tua».

(Si accorge con piacere
che è ancora e che sarà
quello che era,
sempre uguale: un bambino

who stamps his feet
and shouts : "That's not right!")

"You might even believe it.
But later on ...you'll be sorry."

The sharp strokes
the sound you hear
of the alarm clock
that ticks away
the rite of washing away the dirt
in the neat border line of your room
behind closed doors
in the dark, the privacy that's yours.

"You're welcome. Hello.
Really...No, I got it. Your call
is no bother at all."

The pleasure of exploding,
a moment of abandon
after the long suppressing,
the flight, almost, from yourself.
The fine technique
the downright art
of sneezing...

(He doesn't actually
like kids very much.
He always pictures them in his mind
as dirty and smelly, kinds
of small monsters
who ruin everything they touch.)

che pesta i piedi
e grida: «Non vale!».)

«Magari, tu ci credi.
Ma, poi... uno si pente».

I colpi secchi,
il suono che si sente
della sveglia
a scandire il rito
del pulito, nel chiuso
ordinato dalle porte
nel buio, nel privato.

«Ma si figuri. Pronto.
Anzi... No, l'ho avuto.
Non è un disturbo affatto».

Il gusto dello scoppio,
il cedimento e l'abbandono
dopo aver tenuto,
la fuga quasi da sé.
La tecnica sottile
l'arte, addirittura,
dello starnuto...

(A lui, i bambini
un po' dispiacciono.
Li pensa sempre
sporchi e puzzolenti,
piccoli mostri
che toccano e rovinano.)

"Listen, it's tough.
Do you understand that?"
...with the echo that
gathers them,
onto the stage.
Figures in the vague,
flat ghosts
clad in plaid, slippers
and hot-water bottles.

"Criminals. They should be
locked up for good
or put to death."

(He killed so many
only with his thought.
He shouted: "It serves you right,
you swine."
He is the murderer, boasts
about it, the torturer
of his enemies.
Without losing an inch,
it would seems,
of the esteem
he lavishes on his own life.)

"...but learn
not to go too far,
so you don't get burned."

The bedroom's
Chippendale,
with a chest of drawers
and small armchairs. There's

«È dura, senti. Ma
lo vuoi capire?».

… con l'eco che,
a raccolta, li chiama
sulla scena.
Figure nell'opaco,
fantasmi sgonfi
con plaid, pantofole
e borse d'acqua calda.

«Delinquenti. Da
rinchiudere per sempre
o da ammazzare».

(Ne ha uccisi tanti
col pensiero.
Ha gridato: «Porco,
ti sta bene».
È l'assassino, se
ne vanta, l'aguzzino
dei suoi nemici.
Senza che si perda
un dito della stima
che riserva
sulla sua vita.)

«… ma senza esagerare.
Per non esserne scottato».

La camera da letto
è in stile chippendale,
con il comò
e le poltroncine.

a dressing-table
and a big wardrobe.

"What do you have in mind?
Say it, please."

Of pleasant woods here,
only an outline, a trace
of hedges on the wallpaper.
                            Held
in the limited space
inside, in the dark abyss.
Surrendered
                                 swollen enormity
that enfolds and kneads
turgid pulp,
                        soft
cream that spreads warm stench,
humor down from the gurgling
bundle. The fullness
that empties. Beaker
                              ceiling-light
that dangles and holds fast,
yields and contracts.
Basin of soft cream
spineless octopus
                       cascade.

(Maybe 'cause when he was small
he dreamed of assess, bellies
and big tits,
and he was good at drawing them
and popular for it.

Ha una toilette
e un grande armadio.

«Che cosa hai in mente?
Dillo, per favore».

Di lieti boschi, qui,
solo un contorno, di siepi
il segno, alle pareti.
Nel circoscritto spazio
                    presi
dentro, nel buio anfratto.
Arresa
        gonfiata enormità
che avvolge e impasta
turgida polpa,
            crema
frolla che spande caldo afrore,
umore giù dal groppo
che gorgoglia. Il pieno
che si svuota. Ampolla
                    plafoniera
che pende e che consiste
che cede e in sé ritira.
Vasca di panna soffice
molle polipo
            cascata.

(Sarà che lui da piccolo
sognava culi, e ventri
e seni dilatati,
ed era bravo a disegnarli
e lo cercavano per questo.

For him they counted for what they were,
no need of a body or a head.)

...the sides, the squares
in the kingdom, in the warp
of cage and chessboard.
Enchantment glows
on the highest wire,
on the crest of the court's nest.
For the attention
of maids and whores.

"Like this, don't move.
It's only for a moment."
"Stop it, let me go. What are you doing?
Watch out or I'll scream."
"You should be grateful
for what I'm teaching you."
"Oh God. What happens
if Madam hears."

The bathroom's narrow,
with a mirror

on the medicine chest
and the washbasin on the bidet.
Between window
and tub,
the washing-machine
and a shoe-rack.

"Don't think about it. Keep
busier. That way you'll
always have something to fall back on."

Per lui valevano da soli,
senza il resto di un corpo
o di una testa.)

… i lati, le caselle,
nel regno, nell'ordito
di gabbia, di scacchiera.
Ferve l'incanto
sul filo più sospeso,
sulla cresta del nido
della corte. Per la cura
di serve e di puttane.

«Così, stai ferma.
È un attimo soltanto».
«Mi lasci, su. Che fa?
Guardi che grido».
«Dovresti ringraziarmi
per quello che ti insegno».
«Oddio. Ma che succede,
se sente la signora…».

IL bagno è stretto,
con uno specchio
ad armadietto
e il lavandino sul bidè.
E, tra la vasca e
la finestra, la lavatrice
e una scarpiera.

«Non ci pensare. Datti,
più da fare. Così ti resta
sempre qualcosa a cui
ti puoi attaccare».

(However, it seems to him
that women like bastards better,
and lose their heads for them only.
That the others
waiting there lonely
not even a nod,
and despite their good intentions,
count only
as last-ditch solutions.)

"Be open with us.
What's the matter with you?
Let your family advise you."

...yes, of those livid flashes,
that spread
like capillaries
over pale skin.

The sideboards and the hanging
shelves on the wall,
not real wood at all,
in the narrow kitchen. The sink
under the window
and the fridge that covers
a third of the door-space.

"Time passes so fast.
And everything ...Hello. Ages."

The slice of melon
almost melts in the mouth.
it's just full, perfectly ripe.

(Però gli pare che
alle donne piacciono
se sono mascalzoni,
e solo con quelli
perdono la testa.
Che gli altri, pronti,
neppure a un cenno,
alle intenzioni
contino infine
come soluzioni.)

«Ma apriti con noi.
Cosa ti manca? Lascia
che ti consiglino
i tuoi cari».

... sì, di quei lampi
lividi, che si propagano
come capillari
sulla pelle bianca.

La credenza
e i pensili finto legno
alla parete, nella stretta
cucina. Il lavello
sotto la finestra
e il frigidaire che occupa
un terzo della porta.

«Il tempo passa in fretta.
E tutto... Pronto. Invecchia...».

La fetta del melone
quasi si scioglie:
è piena, fatta

Let it slide
on the tongue,
thinking of you meanwhile
cruelly being in command.

(He loves his idea of himself,
lives on that
and on his fantasies.
On his ghosts,
on his glory.)

"I know : for you
it doesn't count, doesn't mean a thing.
After all the work we've done
your father and I."

(Quiet and somewhat introverted
faultless,
obsequient to every law.
He'll answer seriously:
"My pleasure, no trouble at all."
Elegant, yes, and quite
polite. Always discreet
and welcomed everywhere.
And yet...far from the stage
he feels
not in a trap
more in defense
as if he wasn't there at all.)

al punto che si deve.
Lascia che slitti
sulla lingua,
pensandoti frattanto
in tutta crudeltà
al posto di comando.

(Ama un'idea di sé,
vive di quella
e delle sue invenzioni.
Dei suoi fantasmi,
della sua gloria.)

«Per te, lo so,
non conta, non è stato.
Con quel che abbiamo
lavorato, io e tuo padre».

(Riservato e un po' introverso
inappuntabile, a vederlo,
ossequiente di ogni autorità.
Lui che risponde serio:
«Ma si figuri, per carità».
Elegante, sì, e gentile
molto discreto sempre
accolto ovunque con favore.
Sia pure ma... lontano
fuori scena, lui si sente,
neppure poi in agguato
e più in difesa, quasi
del tutto assente.)

Like It or Not

"You know, the first love can be the last, Mrs. Napier."
"You're wrong. No, my dear lady, that's not the way it is."
— *Ivy Compton-Burnett*

"Only the tyrant speaks of love."
— *Norman O. Brown*

"You finally got here.
How come ? Where have you been ?"

(And it doesn't help him
to keep busier.
A gesture cannot fill
the void, and the name
of the absence can
hardly do it, or can only
ruffle the surface of the shadows :
the object, meanwhile
that haunts him.)

"It's useless, because
you don't want to understand."
"It's only a mother's love
that never ends."

"You feel, suddenly,
like this, outside yourself."

Motionless, under glass, naked,
the waiting broods

Per amore o per forza

«Il primo amore, sì, può essere l'ultimo, Signora Napier».
«Ti sbagli. No, mia cara, non è così».
— *Ivy Compton-Burnett*

«Solo il tiranno parla d'amore».
— *Norman O. Brown*

«Sei arrivato, finalmente.
Come mai? Dove sei stato?».

(E non gli serve
tenersi più occupato.
Non riempie il vuoto
un gesto, e appena
lo può fare o solo
corrugarne di ombre
il falsopiano, il nome
dell'assenza: l'oggetto,
nel frattempo, delirato.)

«È inutile, perché
non vuoi capire».
«Quello di una madre
è il solo a non finire».

«Uno si sente, a un tratto,
così, fuori di sé».

Fermo, sotto cristallo, nudo
cova l'attesa

                              dry
raw frost of parting , shell
that hides the delicate
block-sheet that
                              cracks
in the meantime. There :
no longer paralyzing.
Drop after drop, it leaks,
turns to a trickle,
                              stream.
And all around, more and more,
it swells, bursts, merges,
                              pours
from the cuts
of the bleeding wound.
In motion, rushing,
full to the brim,
it overflows, uncontained,
                              as it spreads.

"She'll say that it isn't true,
it only seemed that way.
That she made a mistake ."

"You never stay home any more.
You've changed so much…"

"But why me, anyway?
Because he likes me, I hope."

…and there are no
excuses, no real remedy.

          secco
crudo gelo di distacco
guscio che cela il tenero
lastra blocco che,
              intanto,
crepa. Ecco,
non più paralizzante.
Goccia dopo goccia, perde
si fa rivolo
         torrente.
E, intorno, a distesa
gonfia, scoppia, si confonde
e dai tagli
         versa
della ferita sanguinante.
In movimento, in corsa
colmo fino all'orlo
trabocca, incontenuto,
              spande.

"Dirà che non è vero,
che le era sembrato.
Che ha sbagliato".

«Non stai più a casa.
Come sei cambiato...».

"Perché me, poi?
Perché gli piaccio, spero".

... e non ci sono
scuse, non c'è
rimedio vero.

The room is narrow
and long
with shutters
always closed.

"You really like me, then?
Tell me again."

And yet uncertain,
he faithfully goes his way.
Stumbling in the dark,
groping through smoke and haze,
not knowing anything about
today or tomorrow.
It's made of calls,
of cries and signals
we send each other
like life-belts.

"And you won't get tired
of me ? Not even when…"

(He never rests, no.
He's always there.
And demands
of both of them that they
keep voicing confirmation.)

The wall lamp's light
is weak: the shadows
recede
one from another.

La stanza è stretta
e lunga,
con le persiane
sempre chiuse.

«Ti piaccio, allora io?
Dimmelo ancora».

E pur incerto batte,
fedele, le sue rotte.
Incespicando al buio
in mezzo a fumi e nebbie,
senza sapere niente
dell'oggi e del domani.
È fatto di richiami,
di gridi e di segnali
che ci si lancia andando
come i salvagente.

«E non ti stancherai
di me? Neppure quando...».

(Non si abbandona, no.
Sempre, è presente,
e chiama entrambi
alla pronuncia continua
di conferme.)

La lampada a muro
è fioca: le ombre
si allontanano
le une dalle altre.

"Hug me. Come on,
hold me tight."

To that which flows
unstable, hurls itself
onto the other side
beyond the divide
and breaks up, bursts the banks
mingles and swirls
In the same indifferent
                         magma,
to what is hardly
or not at all enough in itself
for an exact state and role
                         of a person,
that has neither time nor space
no history to trace,
except for a step poised
                         for a brief flight,
the unshakable is opposed,
the only commitment
                         the clean
certainty of something unknown,
                         unseen.

*...feeling that you belong
to someone else, and that
someone belongs to you
exclusively, forever.*

A longing for what lasts,
can be kept at all costs,
for willed resistance
to the void.

«Abbracciami. Dai,
stringimi forte».
A ciò che instabile
trascorre, precipita di là
oltre il versante
e schioda, rompe i margini
confonde e impasta
in uno stesso magma
                      indifferente,
a ciò che a poco
o a niente basta per sé
per un esatto stato
                      e ruolo di persona,
che non ha spazio e tempo
che non ha storia
se non di un passo
                      di breve volo,
si oppone l'incrollabile
il solo impegno
                      la certezza
di cosa non saputa
                      non veduta.

... sentire di appartenere
a qualcun altro, e che
qualcuno ti appartiene
per sempre, in esclusiva.

Un desiderio di durata
di tenuta, a tutti i
costi, di resistenza
premeditata al vuoto.

"But meanwhile, why bother
with me ? What have I got ?
What does she see in me
that she couldn't
find better in somebody else ?"

Books on the floor,
strewn everywhere,
and piles of notebooks threatening to fall
behind the curtain
against the wall.

"We'll stay together forever.
And tell each other everything."

The state of bondage :
a kind of chain by which
whether a lot
or just a little
you seek to be bound.
For which you yearn through fear.
That is imposed, without your knowing it,
while you are undergoing it.

"Heads if he's serious,
wants me forever.
Tails if it's just a game
that will soon be over."

...*out of the blue*
a doubt
strikes you.

"Ma perché, intanto,
interessarsi a me...
Cos'ho? Che valgo?
Che non trovasse di meglio
in qualcun altro".

Libri a terra, sparsi
e pile di quaderni
dietro la tenda
contro il muro.

«Staremo sempre insieme.
E ci diremo tutto».

Lo stato di servaggio:
una specie di cintura
cui si tende, tanto o poco,
cui si aspira per paura.
Che si impone, proprio
mentre si subisce.

"Testa, se fa sul serio.
Se mi vorrà per sempre.
Croce, se è solo un gioco
che finirà".

*... un dubbio, a
tradimento,
ti colpisce.*

"You'll see, believe me,
he'll leave me.
It's just a matter of time
until, finally, he'll tire,
lose his desire."

The bookcase
takes most of the space
in the small storeroom, forms a niche
against the window, which
is half-hidden.

(For him they become
mythology. The detonators
of a destiny to which,
he thinks with fear,
there doesn't appear
to be an answer.)

"Are you making fun of me?
Well, then, how much?"
"A lot, honestly. Even more.
Endlessly. I'm mad about you."

In the current use
it's gauged by the hour.
Yet, in the end, it's given
an undetermined value,
like a treasure
measured
in light years...

*...and still
I'm hiding*

"Ma sì, vedrai,
mi lascerà.
è questione di tempo:
quando si sarà tolto,
finalmente, la voglia".

La libreria
ingombra lo stanzino
e, contro la finestra,
forma una nicchia
per metà nascosta.

(Diventano, per lui,
mitologia. Gli inneschi
di un destino che,
di continuo pensa
con timore, poteva
non aver risposta.)

«Mi prendi in giro?
E, allora, quanto?».
«Tanto, sì. Di più.
Infinitamente. Da morire».

Nell'uso suo corrente,
si misura a ore.
Eppure, va a finire
che se ne dà un valore
indefinito, di tesoro,
di spazio d'anni luce...

*... ancora
mi nascondo*

>   *behind the wall*
of light, fruit
of a dream.

"You're different,
the only one in the world."

Called upon
held onto, elusive,
enjoyed, recited
in its being *everything.*

"It's no good like this, no use.
I won't answer."
"But if I really had
to choose…"

The old parquet of the floor
smells of polish
and creaks continually
with every step you take.

"What if they hear in there…
Please wait. I'm scared."

Together. Holding each other's
bodies gently, uncovered
to touch, to taste
                        debased
by eyes, by hands.
A sense lost
                        regained
in a slow falling

     dietro il muro
di luce, frutto
del sogno.

«Tu sei diverso,
unico al mondo».

Chiamato in causa
tenuto, inafferrabile,
goduto, declamato
nel suo essere *tutto*.

«Così non vale.
Non ti rispondo».
«Ma se dovessi
scegliere davvero...».

Il vecchio parquet
del pavimento
odora di lucido
e crepita in continuazione,
ad ogni movimento.

«Se sentono di là...
Aspetta. Dai, ho paura».

Insieme. Tenendosi piano
sul corpo svelato
al tatto, al gusto
    violato
dall'occhio, da mano.
Un senso perduto
    ripreso,
in lenta caduta

of a weight, letting it go
                          from time
to time, it bends
surrendering to its flight.
At the bottom,
stretched out
slipping into a grip, mingling
yielding to the tight bond.

Beauty, I know,
only you exist.

(Still, he cancels it.
Wish it weren't
the thing of hers
he most prefers.)

"But what do you
really think of me?"

(He's left dismayed
by the claim
he has her thoughts
in him, quails
at the idea the feeling
isn't mutual,
that she neglects
the most absolute devotion.)

The rope door-mat
Is between the chair
and the small table's feet,
stretching to meet
the radiator pipes.

di peso, si lascia
      di volta
in volta, si piega
si rende al suo volo.
Nel fondo, nel morso
       distesi
slittati, confusi
arresi alla stretta cintura.

Bellezza, sì lo so,
tu sola esisti

(Eppure, la cancella.
Vorrebbe che non fosse
la cosa che di più
lo attira in lei.)

«Ma cosa pensi, tu,
di me, poi, veramente?».

(Rimane sconcertato
di fronte alla pretesa
di avere in sé presenti
i suoi pensieri.
Teme di non essere
del tutto ricambiato,
che lei trascuri
la più assoluta dedizione.)

Lo stuoino di corda
è tra la sedia
e i piedi del tavolino,
fin sotto ai tubi
del radiatore.

"What's wrong with you?
Don't you want to?
Don't you like it any more?"

It often happens
normally or by mistake
that every living being
in a state of maturation
is conditioned
in his functions
by the sensations
of pain or gratification.

"Nothing, I'm telling you.
It's not that I'm refusing."

"But you're not answering...
See, you stay there speechless."

"It's hard to believe but
I'm relieved
the minute I go out,
as soon as I leave her."

(He's haunted by the desire
to be in the presence
of the body he loves,
but after having seen it,
and touched it over and over, then
he's forced to admit to his regret
that he's fed up
and in his mind he has already
slipped into the act

«Cos'è che hai?
Non vuoi? Non ti va più?».

Avviene di sovente
per norma o per errore
che ogni essere vivente
in stato di accadere
sia condizionato
nelle sue funzioni
dalle sensazioni
di dolore o di piacere.

«Niente, ti dico.
Non è che mi rifiuto».
«Ma non rispondi...
Vedi, resti muto».

"È incredibile, però
mi sento sollevato
appena uscito,
appena l'ho lasciata".

(Lo incalza l'ansia
di stare alla presenza
del corpo amato
ma, dopo averlo visto
e più e più toccato, è
con dispetto costretto
a riconoscersi saziato
e già con il pensiero
è scivolato
all'atto di lasciarlo

of leaving it
so as to be in fact
on the point of finding it again.)

"It's strange yet true
the relief that
I feel for a moment
as soon as he's gone."

*...like this, open
swollen, pale,
the wound, even though
no longer bleeding.*

The wall is oozing
dampness :
it's all rough
with crusts
so that the pictures
can't hang straight.

"Come on, put your hand in mine."
"There it is, caught in the noose
that holds it fast."
"Swear you won't ever
leave it for another one."

per essere di nuovo
sul punto di trovarlo.)

"Strano, eppure
è vero il sollievo
che provo, per un po',
appena se ne è andato".

… così, aperta
gonfia, illividita,
anche se non più
del tutto sanguinante,
la ferita.

La parete trasuda
umidità:
è tutta ruvida
di croste
che fanno sollevare
i quadri.

«Dai, metti la tua
nella mia mano».
«Eccola, presa nel
laccio che la tiene».
«Giura che mai, per
nessun'altra, la lascerai».

The Siege of Constantinople

"You think I'm hiding something from you, oh my disciples. But there is nothing that I am not telling you, in truth."
—*Confucius*

"I had bad teachers. It was a good school."
— *Arnfrid Astel*

...the dreadful cave,
full of darkness
that stings the eyes,
of our uncertainties
about the targets.

A limitless horizon
that you don't touch,
whose circuit and distance
escape you.

"Beyond the known lands,
they thought, lay
the seat of the blessed
people..."

They have already tried,
with wine, brawling and
love.
But they're bored to tears:
they don't leave
the confined of the room

L'assedio di Costantinopoli

«Pensate che vi nasconda qualcosa, o miei discepoli... Ma non c'è nulla ch'io non vi dica, in verità».
— *Confucio*

«Ho avuto cattivi maestri. È stata una buona scuola».
— *Arnfrid Astel*

... l'orrida caverna,
piena di buio
di punture agli occhi,
della nostra incertezza
sui bersagli.

Un orizzonte aperto
che non tocchi,
di cui ti sfugge
il giro e la distanza.

«Oltre le terre note
pensavano che fosse
la sede del popolo
beato...».

Ci hanno già provato,
col vino con le risse
con l'amore.
Ma si consumano di inedia:
non lasciano
il confine della stanza

Like It or Not

don't go beyond the doors,
through laziness through fear
or unconcern.

(...may he succeed
in rendering into words
the state of waiting
and of lack,
and find relief
even in the absence
whose insubstantiality
he fears every moment.)

To move in large numbers
but each on his own
until nightfall
on the maps, the routes ...
    to quicken the pace
                      upwards
to the winning-post, to the one
who reaches the peak first.
But from the top
                      down below
a thin layer of mist
obscures the view.

In shabby black,
his slightly moon-pale hands
gripping his stick,
the old man the saint
the master of thought
surrounded by his court
of silent stewards,

non passano le porte,
per accidia per timore
o noncuranza.

(... che gli riesca
di rendere a parole
lo stato di attesa
e di mancanza,
che abbia un rilievo
sia pure nell'assenza
ciò di cui si teme, ogni
momento, l'inconsistenza.)

In tanti, muoversi
ma ognuno per suo conto
fino a notte
sulle carte sulle rotte...
affrettare il passo
               verso l'alto
al traguardo, a chi arriva
prima sulla vetta.
Ma dalla cima
             in basso
offusca la veduta
una caligine sottile.

In nero logoro,
le mani un po' lunari
aggrappate al suo bastone,
il vecchio il santo
il maestro di pensiero
attorniato dalla corte
di muti maggiordomi

of prelates who act
as countersong.

(He didn't come here,
it's understood,
so much for the university itself.
It's another idea, basically,
of space and time,
and overturning
of the past.
Curiosity. Something
he'll lose, probably,
before too long,
even if for now
it laves him overwhelmed.)

The entryway is a big
long box.
Some light
comes from the courtyard.
The wall is covered
with graffiti : heads
of Che and
five-pointed stars,
and, over and over, in red
and black paint :
IN THE HEART OF POWER.

"...we know the destiny
of everyone.
Only that of Nausicaa
remains uncertain.
All that we know about her is
that she was a virgin.

di prelati che
gli fanno il controcanto.

(Qua, si rende
conto, non è venuto
tanto per l'università.
è un'altra idea, in fondo,
di spazio e tempo,
un ribaltamento
del passato
La curiosità. Qualcosa
che magari, di lì a poco,
se anche lo lascia
per ora stupefatto,
si perderà.)

L'ingresso è un lungo
scatolone.
La poca luce
gli viene dal cortile.
è tappezzato, il muro,
di disegni: teste
del Che e stelle
a cinque punte
e, ripetuto, con vernici
rosse e nere:
NEL CUORE DEL POTERE.

«… di tutti conosciamo
lo sviluppo.
Solo quello di Nausicaa
resta incerto.
Di lei sappiamo, solo,
che era vergine.

But will it last? Love
or chance or reason of state..."

While he pronounces
loudly
the well-studied formulas,
his lesson,
lifts his forefinger
and modulates his voice laughing,
being on the side, he presumes,
of reason.

(Fear of what lies in wait
but not so much for himself alone
as for her...that later
the encounter with reality will
change and debase
their union or that, even,
he may leave her with
a lower image of himself.
And again, jealousy
that she may expose herself
in some way.
Keeping quiet , ambiguously,
his intention
of choosing for her.)

The staircase is wide and dark.
Yellow-ochre, thick
with damp spots ,
decorated with a variety of things :
UP WITH THE PEOPLE,
NO MORE BIBLIOGRAPHY,
WORKERS AND STUDENTS,

Ma durerà? L'amore o
il caso o la ragion di stato...».

Mentre pronuncia
a piena voce
le ben studiate formule
la sua lezione
e alza l'indice
e modula ridendo
dalla parte, presume,
della ragione.

(Paura di ciò che attende
ma non per sé da solo,
per lei... che poi
l'incontro con la realtà
non muti e adulteri
la loro unione o che,
magari, le consegni di sé
un'immagine inferiore.
E, ancora, gelosia
che lei si esponga.
Tacendo, ambiguamente,
l'intenzione
di scegliere per lei.)

La scala è ampia e buia.
In giallo ocra denso
a macchie d'umido,
istoriato variamente:
IL POPOLO IN ASCESA,
BASTA CON LA BIBLIOGRAFIA,
OPERAI E STUDENTI,

DEATH TO THE GREEDY
MANADARINS OF THE BOURGEOISIE.

The idea, repeated, of
imposing order on the world,
of persisting in the search
for the unknown.
If it were only

a matter of patience.
But f it spares us
a lot of hard work...
Expecting
to find answers
on books, on writings.

Walls thick with volumes
and dust and creaking
of bookshelves
                        all around.
Voices and footsteps,
down at the table
suspended ,
rustling of pages
and elbows and buttons.
Noise in the distance
                        held back
driven out
by paper barriers.
Flows, currents of energy
from one pole to the other,
rebounding from the pages
to the bodies bent over tabletops.
Perpendicularly

Like It or Not • 76

MORTE AGLI AVARI
MANDARINI DELLA BORGHESIA.

L'idea, ripresa, di
dare ordine la mondo
di insistere, alla
ricerca del segreto.
Che sia soltanto
questione di pazienza.
Ma ci risparmi
una fatica...
La pretesa
di chiedere conto
ai libri, alle scritture.

Muri spessi di volumi
e polvere e assestarsi
di legni,
        intorno.
Voci e passi, in basso
al tavolo
        sospesi,
fruscio di pagine
e gomiti e bottoni.
Rumore in lontananza
                trattenuto
respinto fuori
da barriere di carta.
Flussi, correnti di energia
da un polo all'altro
rimbalzando dalle pagine
ai corpi chini sui ripiani.
A piombo

                          In balance
to find out on sheaves of paper
lists reports
of a world that's concentrated
shut as into a box,
squeezed out, distilled.
Everything's blocked
or moving slightly
like seaweed and fishes
                    in an aquarium,
until the thud of a book,
the crash of a chair,
a sneeze.

...despite the effort
that was made
at every step, violating
reasons, sweeping away
the most secure grasps,
nothing is left.
Everything's canceled.

*Amor che a nullo
amato amar perdona...*
But it doesn't explain anything
doesn't belong , doesn't
work, unless
as noise
and pure sound
that reveals nothing else
and gives pleasure
in pronouncing it to oneself,
crumbling it
between the lips.

         in bilico
a pescare, su plichi
elenchi rendiconti
di un mondo concentrato
chiuso in scatola
spremuto, distillato.
Tutto bloccato
o in lieve movimento
di alghe e pesci
            nell'acquario,
fino al tonfo del libro
al crollo della sedia
allo starnuto.

... nonostante lo sforzo
che c'è stato, ad
ogni passo, violando
le ragioni, spazzando via
le prese più sicure,
non resti niente.
È tutto cancellato.

Amor che a nullo
amato amar perdona...
Ma non dà conto
non appartiene, non
funziona, se non
come rumore
e suono puro
che non rileva altro
e dà piacere
nel pronunciarlo a sé
nel triturarlo
tra le labbra.

And ...memory
surrenders, vanishes.

(It happens, has already
happened to him, to believe
or only hope
he's a writer.
He's cautious and rigid
in this exploration :
he auscultates himself, and while
he waits, he's scared. Yes,
he's afraid of the verdict.)

"...could I be mistaken,
then, and be wrong in thinking it
the only expression."

It's a dwelling
here, besides,
as elsewhere,
on the details.

The hall is narrow
and it jars every time
the door slams.
It's a corridor
all divided into rooms,
with windows
down to the floor.

"...from these ras
of tiny kingdoms
with their harems
scribes and pretorians."

E… la memoria
cede, viene meno.

(Gli capita, gli è già
accaduto, di credersi
o solo di sperarsi
uno scrittore.
And …memory
surrenders, vanishes.
È cauto e irrigidito
in questa esplorazione:
si ausculta e, mentre
aspetta, teme. Sì,
ha paura del responso.)

«… che sia un errore,
dunque, e sbagli a ritenerla
l'unica espressione».

È un attestarsi
qui, del resto
come altrove,
sopra i dettagli.

La sala è stretta
e sobbalza ogni volta
allo scatto della porta.
È un corridoio
diviso in stanze,
con le finestre
al pavimento.

«… da questi
ras di regni minimi
coi loro harem
scribi e pretoriani».

*...squeezed now
on all sides,
reduced to a few miles.
It was overrun
by land and by sea
by countless hordes,
by a fleet of ships.*

*It wasn't the corridor,
the bottleneck
of the Thermopylae.*

*Hands that clutch
a livid throat,
pulsing in vain.
On the eyes, on one side,
towers and gilded domes
beyond the walls.
On the other...*

*No memories,
no, no words,
face to face with fear.*

*The fall. The siege
of Constantinople.*

*The idea, at tines,
that what counts is
what has already happened, the rest
of the times, the order
more apparent than ...
the result :
surrendering to things*

*... stretta oramai
da tutti i lati,
ridotta a poche miglia.
Venne investita
per terra per mare
da orde innumerabili
da una flottiglia...*

Non era il corridoio,
il collo di bottiglia
delle Termopili.

*Mani che serrano
una gola livida,
invano palpitante.
Sugli occhi, da una parte,
torri e cupole dorate
oltre le mura.
Dall'altra...*

Niente ricordi,
no, senza parole
di fronte alla paura.

La caduta. L'assedio
di Costantinopoli.

L'idea, a tratti,
che conti quello che
è già stato, il resto
dei tempi, l'ordine
più apparente che...
il risultato:
arrendersi alle cose

as they are, to
their inert motion, as to
support and cover
the emptiness, at least.

"Up above the moon
is the kingdom of the divine
and, underneath,
the human and demonic one.
From ether to earth
the body gets
more and more heavy."

(After all, he doesn't believe
in the clean cut.
Saying no suits him fine
until he can choose.
But the imposed limits,
the blindfold on the eyes
and on memory ...
he can't be involved
by the action that pretends
to illuminate the world,
simulates and keeps silent in the name
of a supposed truth,
of faith.)

The big corridor
doesn't get any light.
It has neon, benches
along the sides,
and low radiators.
Painted slogans all
over the walls,

come sono, al
loro inerte moto, per
reggerne e coprirne,
almeno, il vuoto.

«Sopra la luna
è il regno del divino
e, sotto, quello
umano e demoniaco.
Dall'etere alla terra
il corpo si fa
sempre più pesante».

(Non crede, in fondo,
al taglio netto.
La negazione gli va bene
finché sa scegliere.
Ma i limiti richiesti,
le bende agli occhi
e alla memoria…
Non può coinvolgerlo
l'azione che pretende
di illuminare il mondo
e finge e tace per una
verità presunta,
per la fede.)

Il grande corridoio
non prende luce.
Ha neon e panche
lungo le pareti
e bassi termosifoni.
Scritte di vernice
tutt'intorno,

on which stands out :
NOT MERE FOLLOWERS BUT
SUBJECTS OF HISTORY.

"Main duties,
maybe you never really
thought about it, of all
the priestly orders were,
actually, to prepare
the daily fare
for the gods
and then eat it."

To reduce and hone it,
with progressive refining
and then to let it drop
to the bottom, bankrupt
and so be it. But ...
not even this, in the end,
is the way.

(He's afraid that, remaining
in a defense position
in front of many things,
he won't succeed in telling them
for what they are
and that he can succeed
only if he leaves
an open field
between himself and them.)

su cui campeggia:
NON GREGARI MA
SOGGETTI DELLA STORIA.

«Occupazioni principali,
magari non ci avete
mai pensato, di tutti
gli ordini sacerdotali
erano, sì, ogni giorno
di preparare il pranzo
per gli dei
e poi mangiarlo».

Ridurre assottigliarlo,
in progressivo affinamento
e poi lasciarlo andare
a fondo, bancarotta
e così sia. Ma...
non è, poi, la via
neppure questa.

(Teme che, restando
in posizione di difesa
di fronte a molte cose,
non si riesca a dirle
per ciò che sono
e che si possa farlo
solo lasciando, tra sé
e loro, il campo aperto.)

Notable Results

" …yes, the sublime maxims promote life."
— *The Minister of Education*

"It is not us who succeed in changing things
in accordance with our desire; little by little
it is our desire that changes."
— *Marcel Proust*

"Careful ! Get going,
don't waste time.
Have you done your homework?
Are you through studying?"
"And then…"
"Don't run around.
Don't act silly."
"Phooey."
"Don't misbehave."

"Yes, it looks like
a ghost at this hour."
"A derelict ship."

Light in the mirror and a handle. But
in the wardrobe's dim depths, close-packed
rolled up, stacked
inanimate, piles
of folded white laundry,
in coils and cylinders snaky
against the dry foul-smelling plywood
creaky, scaling,

Prodotti notevoli

«... sì, le sublimi massime promuovono alla vita»
— *il Ministro della Pubblica Istruzione*

«Non siamo noi che riusciamo a cambiare le cose conforme al nostro desiderio, poco a poco è il nostro desiderio che muta».
— *Marcel Proust*

«Sta' attenta. Cammina,
non perdere tempo.
Li hai fatti, i compiti?
Hai finito di studiare?».
«E poi...»
«Non andare in giro.
Non fare l'oca».
«Uffa».
«Non comportarti male».

«Sì, sembra un fantasma
a quest'ora».
«Una carcassa di nave».

Luce in specchio e maniglia.   Ma
nell'opaco fondo dell'armadio,
come stipato in sé ravvolto
e inanimato, accatastarsi in pieghe
di candido bucato,
a liste a rullo a serpentina
contro il secco compensato
maleodorante a scaglie scricchiolante,

seemingly in holiday finery
and preserved intact on its way
motionless,
sealed in shrunken cellophane,
remains substratum pile-dwelling
of useless formulas and figures,
of repeated kinds of gymkhanas,
empty wrapper
wrinkled deflated balloon
crumbled plaster cloak
without dregs or bones,
pleased and self-satisfied, that …
        once free in the wind
swells puffs twists
monster griffon kite
cloth ghost-keel,
pale pearly milk
        white light,
waxen soft body
taken set free.

"…the commitment, in entrusting to you
the new students, the warning ,
the poet's exhortation :
shape *the confident skill
of the bold young people.*"

The curtains are dry
with dust,
through dirty windows
light falls
on the cracked walls.

come bardato a festa
e preservato intatto nel tragitto
fermo rinchiuso in cellofàne
contratto,
         spoglia substrato palafitta
di formule e figure vane
di replicati modi di gincane,
vuoto involucro
rugoso palloncino sgonfiato
intonaco crollato   manto
senza scorie disossato,
di sé pago e contento, che ...
          ma libra al vento
gonfia sbuffa si attorciglia
mostro grifo aquilone
panno chiglia di fantasma,
latte pallido perlato
         bianco luce,
in cera   molle corpo
preso lasciato.

«... l'impegno, nell'affidarle
la nuova gente, il monito,
l'esortazione del poeta:
tempri *dei baldi giovani*
il confidente ingegno».

La tenda è secca
per la polvere,
dai vetri sporchi
la luce passa sui muri
pieni di crepe.

"Sometimes I ask myself
what we're doing here."
"It seems that what you hoped to find
eludes you."

(...sed lex. Therefore
discipline is indispensable
If soldiers didn't obey
the general in the field,
defeat in utter chaos
would be inevitable.)

Yellowish bulbs
dangle from the ceiling
and the desks are rickety,
their tops all marked up.

"...the meaning is to gather,
detach, tear away.
It's said of flowers and fruits,
of bees that sucks pollen.
Of those who enjoy life
but are also consumed by it.
Write, in the margin, the forms :
carpo carpsi carptum carpere."

"You feel like being
somewhere else, meanwhile."
"..may everything
run and pass quickly for you."

Spider webs cover
the dusty grids

«Delle volte mi chiedo
cosa stiamo a fare».
«Sembra che ti scappi
quello che credevi di trovare».

(... *sed lex. La disciplina*
è dunque indispensabile.
Se i soldati non obbedissero
sul campo al generale,
la sconfitta nel caos
sarebbe inevitabile.)

Le lampade pendono giallastre
dal soffitto
e i banchi sono zoppi
con i piani tutti segnati.

«... il senso è cogliere
staccare, strappare.
Si dice di fiori e di frutti,
di api che succhiano il polline.
Di chi si gode la vita
ma anche ne è consumato.
Trascrivete, in margine, le voci:
carpo carpsi carptum carpere».

«Ti viene voglia d'essere
in altri posti, intanto».
«... che tutto corra
e passi, per te, d'un tratto».

Le ragnatele coprono
le griglie polverose

of the big
rusty radiators.

"Speaking of what
has always been said."
"Of books that, really,
no one has read."

"...no, that won't do.
Don't be lazy. Theme:
*Making every suitable
reference...*"

*...thy all agree
the world has changed
and studying has become
the number one problem
for young people.*

*Today, with machines
and the progress of science,
the ignorant man is out of place
in modern civilization...*

*...when we're adults,
what shall we do
what won't we do.
Time presses more and more.*

*...so as to find ourselves again one day
well-adjusted, I trust, to the kind
of world we'll live in.*

dei grandi termosifoni
arrugginiti.

«Parlare di ciò
che sempre è stato detto».
«Di libri che, poi,
nessuno ha letto».

«... no, che non basta.
Non siate pigre. Tema:
*Facendo ogni opportuno
riferimento...*».

... sono tutti d'accordo
che il mondo è cambiato
e che lo studio è diventato
il problema numero uno
per la gioventù.

Oggi, con le macchine
e col progresso della scienza,
l'ignorante è spaesato
nella civiltà moderna...

... di noi
quando saremo grandi,
cosa faremo mai
che cosa non faremo.
Il tempo stringe sempre più.

... per ritrovarci un giorno
a nostro agio, spero,
nel mondo in cui vivremo.

"I saw him yesterday, you know,
leaving school."
"Well, say hello, stop him,
exchange a word with him."

On the floor, dark tangles
of wool and hair
fly up along the walls
at every step.
"I simply cannot
have a conversation with them."
"Everyone keeps his thoughts
to himself."

The blackboard is folded up
against the wall.
The slab
is no longer coal-black
and there's chalk-dust all
along the edges.

Dust pulvis dust,
cloud of dust.
Dust on which to make
the fleeting mark.
In solem et pulverem
Producere doctrinam.
Dust and shadow.
Stinging polishing shaking
in the cone of light
to mingle
in the open doorway.
Trouble and burden left

«L'ho visto ieri
uscendo, sai, da scuola».
«Lo saluti, lo fermi,
ci scambi una parola».

A terra, involti scuri
di lana e di capelli
levitano ad ogni passo
lungo le pareti.

«Non mi riesce di fare
un discorso con loro».
«Ognuno si tiene per sé
i suoi pensieri».

La lavagna è ripiegata
contro il muro.
Il nero della lastra
non è più netto
e una polvere di gesso
sta sui bordi.

Polvere pulvis polvere,
nembo di polvere.
Polvere su cui tracciare
il segno labile.
In solem et pulverem
producere doctrinam.
Polvere ed ombra.
Pungere levigare scuotere
dal cono di luce in fermento
al mescolarsi intorno
nell'apertura della porta.

in the breath
of the heated air.
In dust the grain
that was the beginning.
In dust the grain
that clogs the machine.

"It seems strange, I understand
how it is, and you feel bored
reading it. But it's
just a matter of time,
I give you my word."

In the shadow of the classroom
behind the other girls, way in back,
she's combing her hair and laughing.

"I thought that certain things
only happened to me."
" Only until someone else
tells you about them."

"What's that got to do with it!
The point is : tackle the problem
and from the facts you have in mind
you'll make up the exact picture
of the situation."

(...decisive factor
for the formation, always,
of the moral character.
The young student
must reflect and not be deflected
in the educational process

Molestia e peso lasciati
all'alito dell'aria riscaldata.
In polvere il granello
che fu il principio.
In polvere il granello
che inceppa il meccanismo.

«Appare strano, capisco
come sia, e un senso di noia
vi prende alla lettura. Ma
è solo questione di tempo,
sì, parola mia...».

Nell'ombra dell'aula
dietro alle altre, nel fondo,
si pettina e ride.

«Pensavo che solo a me
accadessero certe cose».
«Finché qualcun'altra
non te lo dice».

«Che c'entra! Il punto,
affronta la questione
e dai dati che hai in mente
componi il quadro esatto
della situazione»

(... fattore decisivo
per la formazione, sempre,
del carattere morale.
Il giovane discente
rifletta e non sottragga sé,
nel processo educativo,

*from the essential
contribution.*)

"Stay home. It's better.
Where is it that you want to go?"
"Wherever I feel like."
"Careful you don't regret it,
we love you here."
"So what."
"The world outside is bad,
you don't know much about it."
"I want to see it for myself."
"What else do you need."

"I don't feel the way
writers seem to feel."
"Maybe they're weird
too many centuries away from us."

They're scribbling something quickly
in their notebooks, giggling,
then reading it together.

"…every intention, the will,
on the verge of happening.
Also destination and necessity.
Understand? *At tamen fiet
quod futurum est.*"

She rests her chin
on another girl's shoulder
and keeps laughing.
The shadow is even thicker
during the lesson.

*al contributo
che è essenziale.)*

«Sta' a casa. È meglio.
Dov'è che vuoi andare?».
«Dove mi pare».
«Guarda di non pentirti,
qui ti vogliamo bene».
«Questo, che c'entra».
«Fuori il mondo è cattivo
tu che ne sai…».
«Voglio vederlo io».
«Qui non ti manca niente».

«Non sento cose simili
a quelle degli autori».
«Forse è gente strana,
lontana troppi secoli da noi».

Scrivono in fretta qualcosa
sul quaderno, ridendo,
e lo rileggono insieme.

«… ogni intenzione, la volontà,
nell'imminenza di un accadere.
Anche destinazione, necessità.
Capite? At tamen fiet
quod futurum est».

Le appoggia il mento
sulla spalla e ride ancora.
L'ombra è più fitta
durante la lezione.

From the cloth from the shadow
the milky larva
of what will be
proceeds imperceptibly,
support and spectre
sign faint resemblance.
Letting yourself go to the shadow
as though balancing
from which to discover light.
To shake yourself, begin again
in the slow state of contact.
Sweet electric liquor,
loose sap.
The dark desire
unfolds and is enveloped,
pushes and pursues,
the sense of an event
that never comes to pass.

"…the rule? Once you see it applied
then, certainly, you'll find
the lesson fixed in your mind."

"I know what he wants
from the way he looks at me."
"It would be enough just for once
to hear him say he isn't sure."

She braids her hair
and, looking down, from
time to time she drops her pen
on the desk.

Dal panno dall'ombra
impercettibile procede,
appiglio e spettro
indizio parvenza lieve,
la larva lattiscente
di quello che sarà.
All'ombra lasciarsi
come in bilico
da cui scorgere luce.
Scuotersi riprendere
nel lento stato di contatto.
Dolce liquore elettrico
linfa disciolta.
Svolge e ravvolge sé
spinge e rincalza
lo scuro desiderio,
il senso di un evento
che non si compie mai.

«... la regola? Vediamola
applicata e avrete, allora sì,
fissata a fondo la lezione».

«So da come mi guarda
quello che vuole da me».
«Mi basterebbe, una volta,
sentirgli dire che è incerto».

Si intreccia i capelli
e, abbassando lo sguardo,
lascia cadere a intervalli
la penna sul banco.

Powerful father
arbitrary rule
master who grasps
and holds up the threads
who moves and sustains
control and permission.
Absent father
distant sun
unknown occupation
pressing puzzle
different and stranger
limit finish end.
Shining father
thought about, dreamed of,
held only by the hand,
returned warrior
briefly disposed to stay
to play to speak for once
papa dad.

"It's here studying
learning the rules of the game,
that you'll have a way to know
and prove yourselves later in life."

"They don't know what to say,
rotate the same few words in a different way."
"The keep repeating the phrases
I've heard for ages."

"Don't think about it. You're only
sick : you're tired, worn out."
"But if I feel okay...They're
my problems. Leave me alone."

Padre potente
arbitrio comando
signore che prende
che regge le fila
che muove e sostiene
dominio e licenza.
Padre che è assente
sole lontano
ignoto mestiere
enigma che incalza
diverso e straniero
limite termine fine.
Padre splendente
pensato e sognato
tenuto soltanto per mano
guerriero tornato
per poco disposto a restare
giocare parlare una volta
babbo papà.

«È qui, studiando
imparando le regole del gioco,
che avrete modo di sapere
e di affermarvi nella vita».

«Non sanno che dire,
un giro di poche parole».
«Ripetono ancora le frasi
che ho sempre sentito».

«Non ci pensare. Stai solo
male: sei stanca, esaurita».
«Ma se sto bene... Son
cose mie. Falla finita».

"They're all fancies. You'll see
they'll pass with a remedy."

Mother smiles
in the whirl of words,
in the sun that, in the evening,
stagnates in the dust
on the desks.

"School means everything to her,
my little girl."
"The only thing a woman needs
is a smattering of knowledge."
"For me it's discipline
that matters most."
At the back of the schoolroom
from the dimly glimpsed group of figures
she looks around
with an air of complicity.

"They're boys and girls and they demand
certainties about their futures."
"She'll see for herself
if ever she has children."
"…I wouldn't say so
but she is very happy
with you, believe me."

"She's still a little girl.
In spite of what goes on
in today's world."
"I've always told her
not to run risks."

«Tutte manie. Vedrai che,
con una cura, ti passerà».

La madre sorride
fra i giri di parole
nel sole che di sera
ristagna sulla polvere
dei banchi.

«È tutta per la scuola
la bambina».
«Vale per una donna,
darle un'infarinatura».
«Prima di tutto, metto
la disciplina».
Nell'aula fonda,
dal gruppo incerto delle figure,
si guarda in giro
con aria di complicità.

«Sono ragazzi e vogliono
certezze per il futuro».
«Vedrà anche lei
se avrà dei figli mai».
«… non lo direi, ma
sta benissimo
con lei, glielo assicuro».

«È ancora una bambina
Con quello che succede
oggi nel mondo».
«Le ho detto sempre
di non esporsi».

"Not to get involved
in certain things."

A few hasty words
and an unfeeling laugh,
while the light drowns
swallowed by the ceiling.

"It's a matter of
good sense, really.
Take it from me:
what really counts,
let me tell you,
is experience."

Mother matrix
shell from which are stripped
the viscera
vulva dark cave
nacreous shell
sheath case.
Mother stepmother
knot iron wire
twisted cord
hawser end
cable reed copper thread.
Mother godmother
post to which the series cleaves
base prop
wand that guides
oar bar tiller.
To get enmeshed
stretch break
the tangle.

«Che non si metta in mezzo
a certe cose».

Poche parole in fretta
e un riso secco,
mentre la luce annega
inghiottita dal soffitto.

«È una questione,
ecco, di buonsenso.
Dia retta a me:
quello che conta,
permetta che glielo dica
io, è l'esperienza».

Madre matrice
guscio da cui si spoglia
il viscere
vulva oscura caverna
madreperlacea conchiglia
fodero guaina.
Madre matrigna
nodo filo di ferro
corda ritorta
capo di gomena
cavo canna filo di rame.
Madre madrina
palo a cui tiene la serie
base puntello
bacchetta che guida
remo spranga timone.
Annaspare nel filo
tendere frangere
districare l'involto.

"What good is it?
It's a practical
and quite natural exercise.
Solfeggio is boring
and monotonous too,
but if you
want to learn to play…"

The door opens
and a porter
comes in with a directive.

(…not only a guarantee
of peace for Europe,
a seal of everlasting union
of lives and destinies ,
in a single history
and a single civilization.
Mazzini's dream…)

"She'd like me sometimes
to repeat her words."
"She wants me to confide
in her, in order to control me."

"It makes me sick…when
I'm not hungry. No, I don't like it."
"Eat, it's good for you.
What did you do at school?"
"When…this morning?
Ugh, nothing. A waste of time."
"What do you mean, nothing? And calm down.
Must you grumble at everything I say."

«A che vale?
È un esercizio pratico
del tutto naturale.
Anche il solfeggio
è noioso ed uguale,
ma se si vuole
imparare a suonare...»

S'apre la porta
ed entra un bidello
con la circolare.

(... *non solo garanzia*
di pace per l'Europa,
suggello di eterna connessione
di vite e di destini,
in una storia sola
e in una civiltà.
Il sogno di Mazzini...)

"Le piacerebbe, a volte,
ch'io ripetessi le sue parole".
"Cerca la confidenza
per controllarmi".

«È uno schifo... senza
fame. No, non mi piace».
«Mangia, che ti fa bene.
Che avete fatto a scuola?»
«Quando... Stamattina?
Niente, uffa. Una scemenza».
«Come niente. E stai composta.
Sbuffa, sì, la poverina».

"The usual, the same old things.
I don't like it and I don't want it."
"Swallow your food and sit up straight.
Are you doing it on purpose? Closer."

"Well, then, what conditions?
How, when, why...
You can't ignore the way
and not know the reasons."

The classroom 's dark,
from the opaque globes up there
the lights reach down
only to mid-air.

"...maybe
even nicer.
But try to understand
the exact way to say it."

She opens the notebook
While looking at her friend,
reads without stopping to take a breath.

*"Life is a ball .
you immerse it
and it comes up again."*

*"Life is a tramp
it goes on its way aimlessly."*

*"Life is dirty water.
It's everything and nothing."*

«Al solito, le stesse cose.
Non mi va, non lo voglio».
«Manda giù, stai diritta
Lo fai apposta? Più vicina».

«Che condizioni, allora?
Come, quando, perché...
Non puoi ignorare il modo
e non sapere le ragioni».

La classe è buia:
dai globi opachi
le luci non scendono
che a mezz'aria.

«... magari
anche più bello.
Cercate, per capire,
l'esatta formula di dire».

Apre il quaderno.
Guardando la compagna,
legge senza respirare.

«*La vita è una palla:
la immergi e torna a galla*».

«*La vita è vagabonda
e va senza intenzione*».

«*La vita è acqua sporca.
È tutto e non è niente*».

Living life state
patent latent
action function
diaphragm of nothing
from nothing
diastolic muscle.
Wandering life state
inciting restraining
action reason
link chain

systolic muscle.
Flowing life state
stagnant running
action separation
part blend mixture
combination.

"You know, the program…
there's a higher plan.
Nothing is born from nothing."

"See you soon then."
"Goodbye, professor."

The row of broken clothes-hooks
in the long hall.
The papers and cigarettes butts all
over the floor.

"You've probably noticed too
that it's strange."
"Little by little you
feel in some ways so different."

Vita vivente   stato
patente latente
azione funzione
diaframma del nulla
dal nulla
muscolo diastole.
Vita vagante   stato
incitante inibente
azione ragione
nesso catena
muscolo sistole.
Vita fluente   stato
stagnante corrente
azione scissione
parte mischia miscuglio
combinazione.

«Sa, il programma...
C'è un piano superiore.
Niente nasce da niente».

«Arrivederci, allora».
«Buongiorno, professore».

La fila degli attaccapanni
rotti, nel lungo
corridoio. Le carte
e i mozziconi, a terra.

«Te ne sarai accorta,
anche tu, che è strano».
«Piano piano, ti senti
in parte, così, diversa».

Flood that carries you off
that bends takes apart
from bank to bank
that falls that jumps.
Wave that seizes
plummets and overflows
that pours out and merges
spills over
that disperses envelopes
combines.
Floating waving.

"It's a wide sea
and you sail in it every day."
"Until you find a piece

"O.K. Let's hurry up.
It's late."
"It's late your eye!
Considering what's waiting for us…"

"With luck maybe
someone won't show up today."

Piena che porta
che piega che smonta
da sponda a sponda
che cala che salta.
Onda che prende
che piomba e dilaga
che versa che fonde
che spande
che dissipa avvolge
congiunge.
Galleggiando fluttuando.

«È un mare grande
of solid ground on which to stay."
e ci si naviga ogni giorno».
«Finché non trovi
un po' di terraferma».

«Dai, sbrighiamoci
che è tardi».
«È tardi, un corno!
Con quello che ci aspetta…».
«Chissà che non sia assente
qualcuno stamattina».

OUTSIDE THE BODY

"There is, in man, a natural tendency to distance himself from his body and remove its functions from himself."
— *Jonathan Swift*

"Our body has this defect, that the more cares and comforts are lavished on it, the more it discovers necessities and needs."
— *Teresa di Lisieux*

"The whole thing then,
would be a big mistake."
"If it's by chance or
a higher plan, I can't make out. But,
for sure, flawed and pain-filled."

*The unknown takes
One step back and goes
Forward endlessly.*

"Or, at least, a feeling
of oblivion…How shall I say.
a kind of drowning."

"May it sink to the bottom,
lost its bearings,
and run away."

There doesn't seem to be
a history in life,

All'infuori del corpo

«C'è, nell'uomo, una tendenza naturale ad
allontanarsi dal corpo e a rimuovere d
a sé le sue funzioni».
— *Jonathan Swift*

«Ha il nostro corpo questo difetto, che
più gli si prodigano cure e conforti, e
più scopre necessità e bisogni».
— *Teresa di Lisieux*

«Sarebbe, quindi,
tutto un grande errore».
«Non so se un caso o
un piano superiore. Ma,
certo, nel difetto e
nel dolore».

*L'ignoto arretra
un passo e avanza
all'infinito.*

«O, almeno, l'impressione
di un oblio... Che so,
di un annegare».
«Che cada a fondo
smarriti gli orizzonti,
e corra via».

Pare che al mondo
non ci sia una storia,

things aren't clearly defined,
from a certain point on, at least, you find
everything seems to happen by inertia
or the pressure of a void
acquiring motion and space
as the days succeed each other
till it's filled.

"Be careful, of course,
where you go. Follow the trail
and don't be led astray.
It doesn't matter if you fail,
especially in what you know.
'Cause the real mystery
lies right in full sight."

*...if you don't lose,
you don't win either.*

It's empty it's nothing,
the dive is endless,
out of shade
                                    shadow,
the body doesn't surface
                                    a voice thrusts
out of water,
each one
                                 hugs
the part of himself that shows
picturing the rest hidden below
stitches the edges
around the gap
imagining the form
that comes only once

che manchino contorni
definiti, che tutto
avvenga, da un certo
punto almeno, per inerzia
o per pressione di un vuoto
che acquista moto e spazio
nel procedere dei giorni
fino a farsi pieno.

«Attento, si capisce, a
dove vai. Segui la pista
senza cedere agli abbagli.
E non vale se sbagli,
meno che mai nel noto.
Perché il mistero
vero è proprio in
ciò che è a vista».

... se non si perde,
neppure si conquista.

È vuoto è nulla
il tuffo non finisce
ombra da ombra
                 tiene
il corpo non risale
                 voce dall'acqua
spinge
di sé ciascuno
                 stringe

la parte che ne affiora
e finge il resto immerso
ne cuce i lembi
ai bordi della falla

in blood and mud
dissolved into being
and up from the bottom
only upside down
deep in the depths
                              inter
urinas et feces
under a dim light
through dressings and instruments
out and afloat
                              nascimur.

Within the space
of theory,
identity (mine?)
almost the result of entries
at the registry.

Life : state of
confused situation,
attempted relation
between what today was
uselessly organized
and what yesterday was
inescapably traced.
Torment of gestures
and intentions,
compromise of words
lived and never accepted.

(He doesn't feel
neither young nor old,

ne immagina la forma
che viene e non ritorna
dentro sangue e fango
in essere disciolto
e su dal fondo
solo capovolto
nel più profondo
                inter
urinas et feces
sotto una luce stanca
per ferri e garze
fuori a galla
            nascimur.

Dentro lo spazio
di teoria,
identità (la mia?)
risultanza
quasi d'anagrafe.

Vita: stato di
confusa situazione,
tentata relazione
tra un oggi
invano organizzato
e quel che ieri ha teso
ineludibile tracciato.
Strazio di gesti
e di intenzioni,
compromesso di parole
vissuto e mai accettato.

(Non si vede né
giovane, né vecchio,

couldn't say if handsome
or homely. He only
feels as if he's in the way
or else he comes near
to completely
disappearing.)

Check-ups, delays,
a seemingly endless wait,
before you finally
take flight.

*...so, on the falling
motion, riding the crest
of that wave...*

" Till you discover
that then, beyond,
there's no shore."

The progressive cancellation
of people we love or knew,
the account that begins
not to balance as due.
The margin reduces
as more gaps appear
in the thinning rows.

"On the other hand,
the dissatisfaction that assails you
is only natural."

non sa se bello
o brutto. Si
avverte come ingombro
oppure si scompare
quasi del tutto.)

Controlli, indugi,
attese a non finire
prima di spiccare
finalmente il salto.

*... così, sul declinare
andante, sul filo
di quell'onda...*

«Fino a scoprire
che poi, di là,
non c'è la sponda».

È la cancellazione
progressiva delle
presenze care o note,
il conto che comincia
a non tornare. Il
margine sempre più
sottile, man mano
che si fanno falle
e vuoti tra le file.

«Del resto, è
naturale l'insoddisfazione
che ti assale».

... for what
you thought
or the memory
of what has been.

(He isn't very fond
of glimpses of nature
unless they're viewed
offstage,
from the right observation post,
at least as safe
as it can possibly
be made.)

"Almost as if I had
to make it better."
"Because, indeed,
it's always disappointing."

In the sign of escape
and of absence,
of the rotten and obscure,
of the kingdom
no sooner won than lost,
of the bloated pig
that gets its throat cut,
of the heap of snow
that melts into nothingness.

(He's obsessed by filth,
by what 's slimy and dark.
Horror-struck
by the very sight of spiders,
bugs.

... per quello che
hai pensato
o nel ricordo
del già stato.

(È che non ama
gli squarci di natura
se non da fuori
del palcoscenico,
da un giusto osservatorio
almeno per il poco
che si possa
presidiato.)

«Quasi dovessi
renderla migliore».
«Perché, in effetti,
è sempre deludente».

Nel senso della fuga
e dell'assenza, del
marcio e dell'oscuro,
del regno perso
appena conquistato,
del porco che si gonfia
ed è sgozzato, del
mucchio di neve
sciolta in niente.

(Ossessione di sporco,
di viscido, di scuro.
Dei ragni, ha orrore
solo a vederli,
degli insetti.

The idea of touching them at all
takes his breath away,
it's like he bumped
into a wall.)

"It happens to lots of people.
They cherish the illusion
Or the hope
of a solution."

Sometimes you get through
one of those passageways :
tunnel or hallway
between inside and out
between empty and full.
A well, a volcanic cone,
a precipice. A border
gorge, it seems.

... *eyes fixed*
on the unknown,
the tone
relaxed, a sudden
spasmodic twitch
of bright red lips
in the waxen face.

A breeze that blows
on everything,
a condensation

L'idea di un contatto
gli mozza il fiato,
è come se picchiasse
contro il muro.)

«Capita a tanta gente.
Con l'illusione, sì,
o la speranza
di una soluzione».

Si incontra a volte
uno di quei passi:
tunnel, corridoio
tra il dentro e il fuori
tra il pieno e il vuoto.
Pozzo, cono di vulcano,
precipizio. Gola, così
pare, di frontiera.

*... lo sguardo fisso
nell'ignoto, il tono
abbandonato, lo scatto
incontrollato di un
labbro rosso vivo
sul volto di cera.*

Un soffio che respira
su ogni cosa,
una condensa di

of breaths and
decomposing matter,
a breath of death
that touches down
in slow damp
fermentation.

"Look, it may well be
just as you say.
But it's boring anyway."

(...through circumstances
make him prefer discretion
and have imposed on him
whatever good taste
and bourgeois vices
he possesses.)

The annoying thing is
that it happens too
when we're not there
Aad, involved meanwhile
in something else,
aren't even aware.

(He knows, he likes
— it must be his way
wholly cerebral —
to keep her shoes on,
at least this one,
with the pointed heel
she carries with her :
he likes to touch it, feel
that he's being trampled.)

fiati e di sostanze
in decomposizione,
un alito di morte
che si posa
in lenta umida lievitazione.

«Guardi, sarà
come lei dice.
Comunque, ci si annoia».

(... nonostante l'ambiente
gli faccia preferire
farther away.
discrezione e gli
abbia imposto quel tanto
di buon gusto,
vizi borghesi.)

La cosa fastidiosa
è che accada anche
quando non ci siamo
e, presi intanto
dentro un'altra storia,
non ce ne accorgiamo.

(Lo sa, gli piace
— sarà il suo modo
tutto di testa —
che lei tenga le scarpe,
almeno una, questa
col tacco a punta
che si porta dietro:
toccarla, intanto,
sentire che lo calpesta.)

It's an odd feeling...
"Come on, scratch
with your claws!"
of taking and prevailing,
having her in his power.

The state of pleasure
in which, while
standing quite still,
you follow with your gaze
someone who's moving
farther away.

Yes, with taste,
with touch and sight,
using his whole
head, hands and lips
and skin...in short,
with his body but
being outside of it.

(Together, again
and always, on stage
making the play come true.
She's at the doctor
with whom she's betraying
her spouse.
She plays the maid
he sleeps with as soon
as the Lady goes out.
He's prone and
she's ready, both willing
to play their parts.)

È un senso strano...
«Dai, gratta
con gli artigli!»
di presa e di potere,
per tenerla in mano.

Lo stato di piacere
in cui, da fermi,
si segue con lo sguardo
qualcuno in movimento
più lontano.

Col gusto, sì,
col tatto e con la
vista, con tutta la sua
testa, mani e labbra
e pelle... insomma,
con il corpo ma
all'infuori del suo
corpo.

(Uniti, ancora
e sempre, sulla scena
che si avvera.
È dal dottore
con cui tradisce
suo marito.
È la cameriera
con cui se l'intende
quando è uscita
la signora.
Incline, lui, e
pronta, lei, insieme
a recitare la commedia.)

It's the acted role
that matters, the one violated
by being spoken.
It's the sacred thing
that by its very nature
becomes the cursed thing.

*...the tiger bites
and scratches. Her tongue
slips off.*

I want you mine,
faithful and
totally dependent.
I want to do
with your life as I please,
without restrictions.
Even if it's against
all reason,
even if I feel
it's a kind of trick,
for fear,
a violence.
However that may be.

Maybe it's a kind
of disturbing interference,
the effect of love
that can't possess entirely,
but keeps you
from letting go.

È la parte detta
e, dicendola, violata
quella che conta.
È ciò che è consacrato
a farsi per istinto
l'oggetto bestemmiato.

*... morde, la tigre,
e graffia. La lingua
che scivola via.*

Ti voglio mia,
fedele a me in
assoluta dipendenza.
Disporre di tutta
la tua vita,
senza misura.
Anche se è contro
la ragione, anche
se sento che è
un inganno, per paura,
e una violenza.
Sia quel che sia.

Sarà il disturbo
di qualche interferenza,
effetto dell'amore
che non può prendere
del tutto, ma che
impedisce di lasciare.

It's the need to guard
your flank, that leaves you
holding on but not resolved
to be involved
completely. En
the weight of skepticism
faced with the evidence
assaulting you that,
no matter what,
everything's fated, sadly,
to come out badly.

"Can you succeed
in writing it,
discovering it ...
the presumed truth
of things?"

The tall white
knight, the only one
of his kind.

It happens quite unplanned
through countless
numbers of forces
in the field,
surprise, the good luck
of a different route,
the descent from
more distant spaces,
the intersection
at the same place.

Necessità di presidiare
un fianco, con la
conseguenza di
tenere senza essere
disposti per intero
ad aderire. E, poi,
il peso scettico
di fronte all'evidenza
che ti assale, che
comunque e sempre
tutto sia destinato
a finir male.

«Si può riuscire
a scriverla, sì, a
trovarla… la verità
presunta delle cose?».

*Il cavaliere bianco
alto, irripetibile
singolare.*

Accade senza piani
per una somma
incalcolabile
di forze in campo,
la sorpresa, la chance
di un altro corso,
la discesa da spazi
più lontani,
l'intersezione
nello stesso punto.

But always lacking
even the time or the way
to start talking.

(He's been in this place before
and who knows
how many more
times he'll be here.
If she weren't there,
there'd be another one instead
to echo what he said.
The solution's here
totally unforeseen, at that,
cynical and cruel,
in admitting that the scene
could change the actors too,
and that he could say
the same things
to other people
with the same conviction.)

"It looked as though,
I don't know, it might be forever …
Crucial."
"In an , you would
have said, eternal union."

The farther on we go
— it's a fact —
the view is turned upside down.

Ma sempre senza
il tempo o il modo
neppure di
attaccar discorso.

(È un posto, questo,
in cui è già stato
e in cui sarà
chissà quante altre volte.
Se non ci fosse lei,
sarebbe un'altra
a fargli eco.
È, qui, la soluzione
magari anche imprevista
cinica e crudele,
nell'ammissione che
la scena possa
mutare le comparse
e che si dicano
con eguale convinzione
le stesse cose
a più persone.)

«Sembrava tale che,
non so, per sempre...
decisiva».
«In una, avresti
detto, eterna
connessione».

Andando, si ribalta
— è noto — la prospettiva.

When standing still
we failed to note in full
the question's only relative.
It's motion, yes, that
puts us into relation
with things and ... makes
far-off objects close
and nearby ones suddenly
not there.

(All of a sudden he's inside
the tunnel
in the dead air
that stings his throat.
So many times
he's been through this before...
and yet, no, it's useless.
to recall,
or anticipate a single time.
He bumps into the wall
and there he finds
in his blind
unchanging course
— mirror of himself
to his shed skin -,
of what he's been,
and how much, after all,
he's changed
against his will.)

So, spontaneously, everyone claims
to be back in a place

E, stando fermi,
sfuggiva in pieno
che è una questione
solo relativa. È
il moto, sì, che
mette in relazione
con le cose e... fa
presenti le distanti
e le vicine subito
vacanti.

(È all'improvviso,
dentro al tunnel
nell'aria morta
che pizzica alla gola.
Tutte le volte
che c'è già passato...
Eppure, no, non vale.
Che lo ricordi,
lo anticipi una sola.
Picchia nel muro
e lì si rende conto,
dentro il percorso
cieco e uguale
— specchio di sé
a una sua spoglia —,
di ciò che è stato
di come, in fondo
e contro ogni sua voglia,
lui sia cambiato.)

Così, spontaneamente,
pretende ognuno
di ritrovarsi al posto

never possessed. The role
he is assigned
fades face to face
with the kind
he plays in his own mind.

...the sweet burden.
And still , the feather plummets
like lead to the abyss.

All at once, the idea
of a motionless void,
of nothingness, the absence
of a sign or trace,
freezes the blood and
makes hands and voices shake.
At the most distant point,
no longer that far off :
at the river's mouth,
only a step, a span away
from the frontier, who, or what,
is there ...to save me
from the fatal jump,
from condemnation.

"In this way, from above
I reached a compromise:"
"With the dream of an accord
in perfection."

And yet, meanwhile,
I bowed to the fact
that I was sailing adrift.

che non ha. La parte
che gli è data dilegua
di fronte a quella
immaginaria.

*... il carico soave.
Precipita però, la piuma,
come piombo nell'abisso.*

All'improvviso, l'idea
di un vuoto, senza moto,
del nulla, dell'assenza
di un segno o di una traccia,
agghiaccia il sangue e
fa tremare mani e voce.
Nel punto estremo e,
ormai, non più lontano:
alla foce del fiume,
a un passo, ad una spanna
dalla frontiera, chi c'è
o cosa... che mi salvi
dal salto, dalla condanna.

«Così, dall'alto
scesi a un compromesso».
«Col sogno dell'accordo
in perfezione».

Eppure, intanto,
arresi all'evidenza
di andare navigando
alla deriva.

About the Author

Born in 1949, **Paolo Ruffilli** attended the University of Bologna, where he studied modern literature. After a period of teaching high school, he became editor with the Milanese publisher Garzanti, and is presently the general editor of Le Edizioni del Leone in Venice. As an editor, he has not only supported contemporary poetry but also shown a scholarly interest in the Italian literature of the nineteenth century, preparing editions of the *Operette Morali* of Giacomo Leopardi, Ugo Foscolo's translations of Laurence Sterne's *Sentimental Journey,* and *Le confessioni d'un italiano* by the poet, novelist, and patriot Ippolito Nievo. Ruffilli has also written a biography of Nievo. He has published criticism in a number of periodicals, and is the regular literary critic of the Bolognese daily *Il Resto del Carlino.*

Since 1972, Ruffilli has published nine volumes of poetry, and has in preparation a further collection and a novel. This collection, *Like It or Not* (*Piccola colazione,* 1987) has enjoyed tremendous success, selling more than five thousand copies in a nation where a sale of one thousand copies for a book of poems is considered quite healthy. The volume has won numerous prizes and was the subject of both a television special and a radio broadcast. An evening devoted to *Piccola colazione* was also held at the 1988 Frankfurt Book Fair, with papers read in Italian, French, German, Spanish, and English.

About the Translators

Ruth Feldman is the author of five books of poetry and fifteen books of Italian translations, all poetry with the exception of Primo Levi's concentration camp stories. In 1999 Feldman and John P. Welle received the Raiziss/de Palchi Book Prize for their translation of Andrea Zanzotto's work *Peasant's Wake for Fellini's Casanova and Other Poems* (U of Illinois P, 1997). She has won the John Florio Prize in England, the Circe-Sabaudia in Italy, and the Italo Calvino Prize in the United States, and her poetry has been translated into Italian, French, and Spanish. The recipient of a Literary Translator's Fellowship from the National Endowment for the Arts, she has lectured and read at many universities in the US and Italy.

James Laughlin was the son of a steel manufacturer, attending Choate School in Connecticut and subsequently Harvard University (BA, 1939). In the mid-1930s Laughlin lived in Italy with Ezra Pound, a major influence on his life and work; returning to the United States, he founded New Directions in 1936. Preferring experimental writers over the more traditional, he published books by an impressive list of writers: F. Scott Fitzgerald, William Carlos Williams, Delmore Schwartz, Vladimir Nabokov, Henry Miller, Lawrence Ferlinghetti, and numerous others. Himself a poet of note and author of numerous books, his work is available in the volume *Collected Poems of James Laughlin* (1992).

BORDIGHERA PRESS is

BORDIGHERA POETRY PRIZE

The bi-lingual prize for poetry, including book publication, is sponsored by the Sonia Raiziss-Giop Charitable Foundation. The prize was established to foster the Italian language among Italian-American poets and to offer publication to the best English manuscript by an identifiably Italian-American poet each year.

Most Recent / Forthcoming

6 (2004) Gerry LaFemina; translated by Elisa Biagini; *The Parakeets of Brooklyn*
7 (2005) Carolyn Guinzio; translated by Franco Nasi; *West Pullman*
8 (2006) Grace Cavalieri; translated by Maria Enrico; *Water on the Sun*

CROSSINGS
An Intersection of Cultures

A refereed series, CROSSINGS is dedicted to the publicaion of bilingual editions of creative works from Italian to English. Open to all genres, the editors invite prospective translators to send detailed proposals.

Most Recent / Forthcoming

16 (2006) Giuseppe Bonaviri; trans. Barbara De Marco; *Saracen Tales*

VIA FOLIOS

VIA FOLIOS is a refereed "small-book" series dedicated to critical studies on Italian and Italian/American culture. VIA Folios also publishes works of poetry, fiction, theatre, and translations from the Italian.

Most Recent / Forthcoming

35 (2005) Bea Tusiani; *Con amore: A Daughter-in-Law's Story of Growing Up Italian-American in Bushwick*
36 (2005) Anthony Julian Tamburri, ed.; *Italian Cultural Studies 2002*
37 (2005) Stephen Belluscio; *Constructing a Bibliography*
38 (2005) Fred Misurella; *Lies to Live By*

ITALIANA

Italiana is a series devoted to the publishing of conference proceedings.

Most Recent / Forthcoming

XI (2005) *Medusa's Gaze: Essays in Italian Renaissance Literature, Art, and Gender Studies. Essays in Honor of Robert J. Rodini*

www.ingramcontent.com/pod-product-compliance
Lightning Source LLC
Chambersburg PA
CBHW070457100426
42743CB00010B/1660